POLITICAL RESISTANCE IN THE CURRENT AGE

BY DUCHESS HARRIS, JD, PHD

WITH MYRA FAYE TURNER

Core Library

Cover image: People protest the racist demonstrations
held in Charlottesville, Virginia, in August 2017.

An Imprint of Abdo Publishing
abdopublishing.com

abdopublishing.com

Published by Abdo Publishing, a division of ABDO, PO Box 398166, Minneapolis, Minnesota 55439. Copyright © 2018 by Abdo Consulting Group, Inc. International copyrights reserved in all countries. No part of this book may be reproduced in any form without written permission from the publisher. Core Library™ is a trademark and logo of Abdo Publishing.

Printed in the United States of America, North Mankato, Minnesota
092017
012018

Cover Photo: Scott Eisen/Getty Images News/Getty Images
Interior Photos: Scott Eisen/Getty Images News/Getty Images, 1; Shannon West/Shutterstock Images, 4–5; Shutterstock Images, 7; Frantic Studio/Shutterstock Images, 10; Everett Historical/Shutterstock Images, 12–13; Rachel Griffith/AFP/Getty Images, 15; Scott Nelson/AP Images, 17; Al Grillo/AP Images, 20; Joseph Sohm/Shutterstock Images, 26–27; Brynn Anderson/AP Images, 29; Red Line Editorial, 32, 39; Erin Scott/Polaris/Newscom, 34–35; Albin Lohr-Jones/Sipa/AP Images, 40

Editor: Marie Pearson
Imprint Designer: Maggie Villaume
Series Design Direction: Claire Mathiowetz

Publisher's Cataloging-in-Publication Data

Names: Harris, Duchess, author. | Turner, Myra Faye, author.
Title: Political resistance in the current age / by Duchess Harris and Myra Faye Turner.
Description: Minneapolis, Minnesota : Abdo Publishing, 2018. | Series: Protest movements | Includes online resources and index.
Identifiers: LCCN 2017947132 | ISBN 9781532113987 (lib.bdg.) | ISBN 9781532152863 (ebook)
Subjects: LCSH: Political development--Juvenile literature. | Civilization, Modern--21st century--Juvenile literature. | Social change--Juvenile literature.
Classification: DDC 909.83--dc23
LC record available at https://lccn.loc.gov/2017947132

CONTENTS

CHAPTER ONE

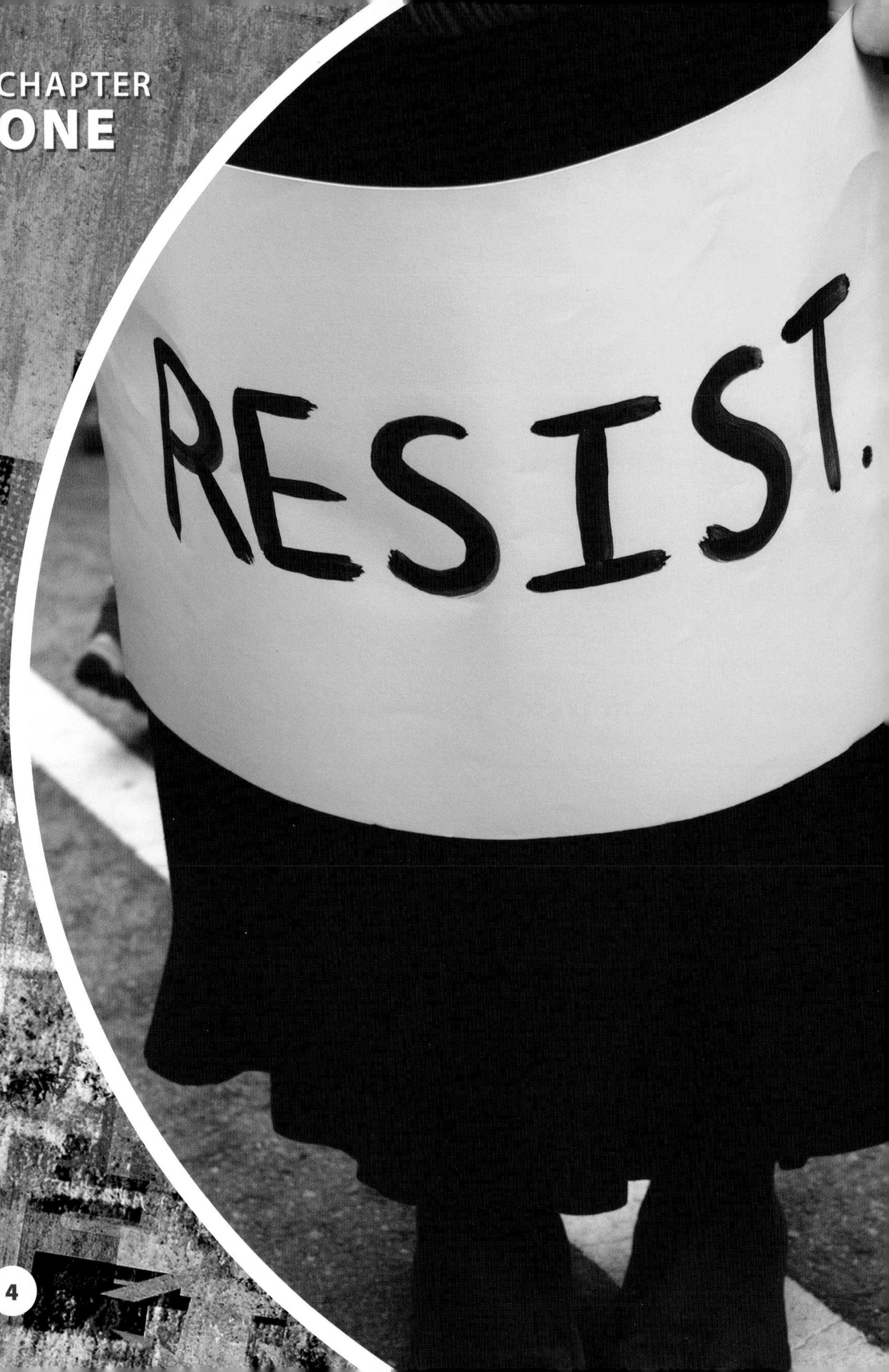

THE WOMEN'S MARCH ON WASHINGTON

n November 8, 2016, Donald Trump was elected president of the United States. His supporters were overjoyed. Other Americans were disappointed. One of them was Teresa Shook, a retired lawyer living in Hawaii. She wondered what would happen if women marched in Washington, DC, around the time of the inauguration in January.

Shook was bothered by some of the things Trump said during his campaign. Critics accused him of racism, sexism, and mocking disabled people. Some felt his

Shook did not think anything would come of her idea, but she ended up inspiring a whole movement.

THE RIGHT TO ASSEMBLE PEACEFULLY

The First Amendment guarantees the right to assemble peacefully. Marches, protests, and rallies are types of assemblies. These events are held in public spaces such as parks. Sometimes, organizers need special permits. Most protesters do not need one. But they must follow certain rules. They cannot block sidewalks. They cannot interfere with traffic. If they need to close streets, they need a permit. They also need a permit if a police escort is required.

proposed policies were harmful. Shook believed Trump's opponent, Hillary Clinton, was more qualified to lead the country.

Shook formed a resistance. She created a Facebook event for the march. Before she went to bed, 40 people said they would participate. The next morning, 10,000 people had signed up. Shook was stunned.

She needed help. Shook asked her Facebook friends to lend a hand.

Protesters filled the streets of Washington, DC. Some carried signs that made their feelings known.

THE MOVEMENT GROWS

Bob Bland, a fashion designer from Brooklyn, New York, had a similar idea. Shook and Bland decided to create one event. The organizers said the march was not against President Trump. It was against his policies.

Bland and three experienced organizers—Tamika Mallory, Carmen Perez, and Linda Sarsour—planned the national event. They named it the Women's March on Washington. They scheduled a rally and march for Saturday, January 21. This was the day after the inauguration. People who could not make it to Washington, DC, created sister marches across the country and world. People in other countries joined the movement.

A SUCCESSFUL MARCH

Approximately 500,000 women, men, and children marched in Washington, DC. Around the world, more than 5 million people protested. They came from all walks of life. They were young and old. They were of many races and ethnicities. People with and without disabilities marched together.

A rally was held near the US Capitol before the march. Speakers included celebrities such as actress Scarlett Johansson. Musical guests included Janelle

Monáe. The marchers carried signs. A sea of pink hats floated down the street. Some people marched for women's rights. Others were concerned about immigration policies. Some worried their health care would be taken away. Others marched for LGBTQ rights and racial equality.

The march was only the beginning. Voters did not have to wait until the next presidential election to make

PERSPECTIVES

IMMIGRATION REFORM

Children born in the United States are automatically citizens. Six-year-old Sophie Cruz is an immigration activist. She worries about her parents. Sophie is a US citizen. Her parents are undocumented. Under President Trump's proposed immigration plan, anyone in the United States illegally could face arrest, detention, or deportation. Sophie was the youngest speaker at the Women's March. In her speech she said, "I also want to tell the children not to be afraid, because we are not alone. There are still many people that have their hearts filled with love."

MARCH 4 TRUMP

On March 4, 2017, President Trump's supporters held a march. They wanted to show their support for the president. The main march was held in Washington, DC. Local marches took place in several US cities. The event was called March 4 Trump. Visit the website below to read more about the event. According to the article, what are some reasons Trump supporters participated?

CBS: MARCH 4 TRUMP RALLIES

abdocorelibrary.com/political-resistance

their voices heard. The focus shifted to local and state elections. Voters could elect politicians they agreed with. The Women's March organizers encouraged participants to continue using nonviolent resistance to protest important issues.

Demonstrators wore pink hats to show their support of women.

CHAPTER TWO

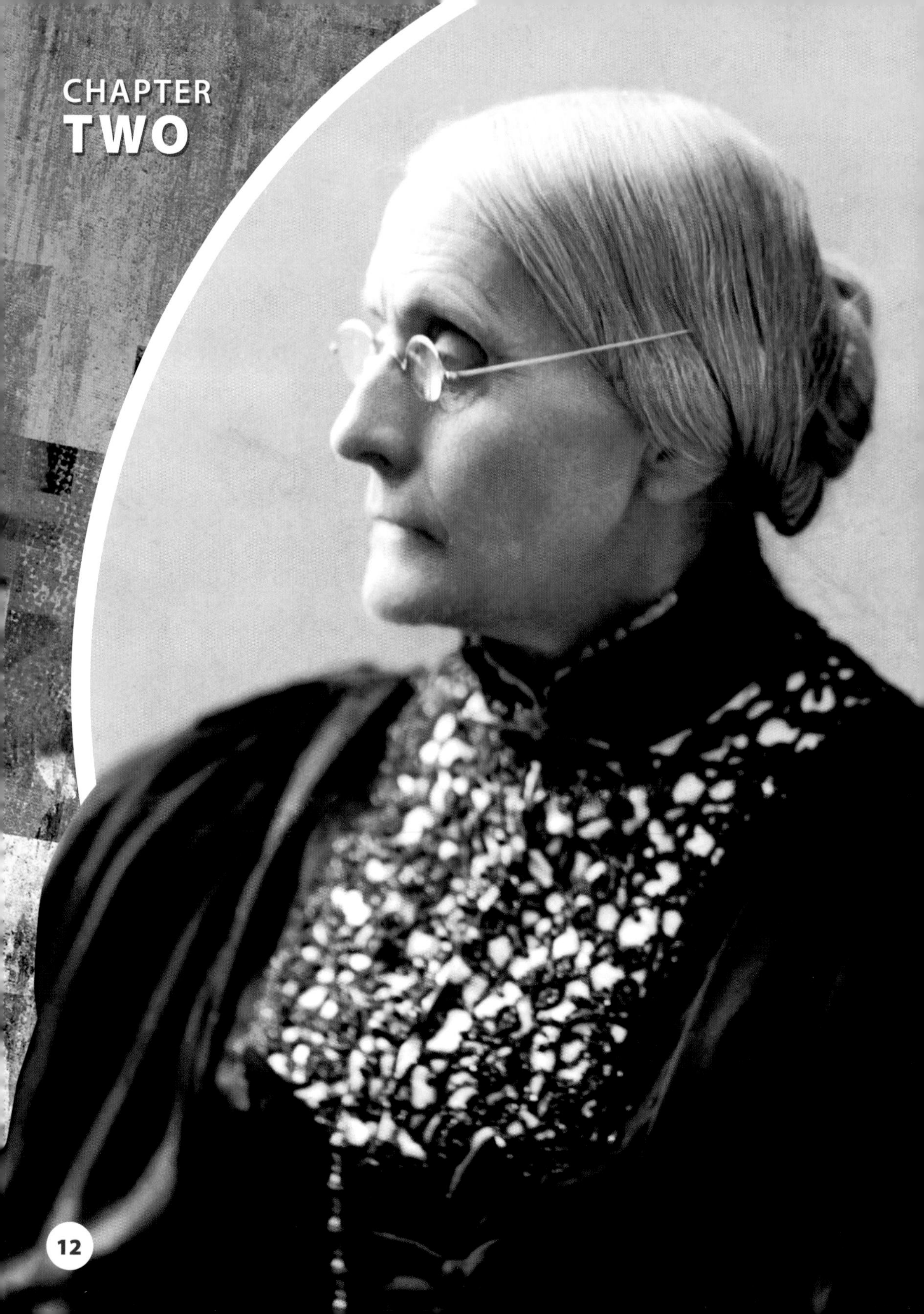

HISTORY OF POLITICAL PROTESTS

Political resistance is not new. In the 1770s, the Sons of Liberty threw 342 chests of tea into Boston Harbor. They were protesting British taxes on things such as tea. They had no say in the taxes. They had no voice in the British government. The Boston Tea Party led to the American Revolutionary War (1775–1783) and the founding of the United States of America.

In the 1800s and 1900s, activists such as Susan B. Anthony pushed for women's right

Anthony helped found the National Woman Suffrage Association, an organization that promoted women's right to vote.

to vote. Because of their work, the 19th Amendment passed in 1920. This allowed women to vote. Civil rights activists in the 1960s held nonviolent protests. They objected to Jim Crow laws limiting African-American rights. This movement led to new laws including the Voting Rights Act of 1965 and the Civil Rights Act of 1968.

RECENT HISTORY

Political resistance has continued into recent history. George W. Bush narrowly defeated Democratic nominee Al Gore in the 2000 election. The election came down to one state: Florida. Florida's count was so close officials recounted the ballots. On November 26, Bush was named the winner of Florida by 537 votes. Gore challenged the results. The case went to the US Supreme Court. On December 12, 2000, the court upheld the official count. Bush won the election.

Some Bush protesters held upside-down flags to show their frustration with the election.

Activists argued the Supreme Court chose Bush, not the voters. Protesters came to Bush's inaugural celebration. Thousands lined the parade route. They claimed the president stole the election. Someone threw an egg at the president's limousine.

The protests continued. On September 11, 2001, terrorist attacks shook the nation. Approximately 2,974 people died in Pennsylvania, New York City, and Washington, DC. The next month, US troops invaded Afghanistan. They were looking for Osama bin Laden. Bin Laden led the terrorist group responsible for the attacks. But bin Laden was not found. Bush worked to prevent future terrorist attacks. On October 26, 2001, he signed the USA PATRIOT Act. This act gave US law enforcement agencies flexibility in handling suspected terrorists. But many Americans criticized the act. They said it allowed the government to invade innocent citizens' privacy. In April 2002, protesters marched in Washington, DC. They opposed the war in Afghanistan and Bush's military policies. The protest was organized

At first many Americans supported the Iraq War because of Hussein's violent policies.

by Mobilization to Stop the War. Seventy-five thousand people participated.

Bush responded to protesters' concerns. He said that even though they did not want war, it was his job to protect American citizens. And he believed there was still a threat. In 2003, Iraqi leader Saddam Hussein did not cooperate with United Nations weapons inspectors. This led Bush to believe Hussein was hiding weapons of mass destruction. The United States invaded Iraq on March 20, 2003. Hussein was eventually captured in 2003. No weapons were ever found. Hussein was executed by Iraqi officials for killing nearly 150 innocent Iraqis in 1982.

In 2004, Bush was reelected. On inauguration day, protesters gathered around the country. Many were angry over the number of people killed in the Iraq War. More than 1,300 US troops had died in the war by 2005. They were also upset about the USA PATRIOT Act. They protested to try to change the direction of the Bush administration. But the Iraq War would last until 2011. The USA PATRIOT Act was not replaced until 2015.

THE OBAMA ADMINISTRATION

The next president also faced resistance. On November 4, 2008, Barack Obama was elected president. He was the first African-American US president. Obama wanted to reform health care. The Patient Protection and Affordable Care Act was signed on March 23, 2010. It is often called the Affordable Care Act (ACA). Critics of the bill did not like that all citizens must have insurance or face a fine. Politicians began working to repeal the ACA. Officials from several states sued the government. They argued the act was unconstitutional.

On November 6, 2012, Obama was reelected to office. People continued to protest the ACA. Republicans wanted to replace it. Health insurance costs had risen. Some people had trouble affording insurance.

RISE OF THE TEA PARTY MOVEMENT

The Tea Party Movement formed in 2009 in response to Obama's policies. Members of the

PERSPECTIVES

THE TERM *OBAMACARE*

Republican lawmakers felt that if they called the ACA Obamacare, Obama's critics would oppose the bill. But in a 2014 interview, Obama said he did not care if people used the term. "I like it. I don't mind," he said.

The tea bags Tea Party protesters wore were a reference to the Boston Tea Party.

movement wanted less government involvement in citizens' lives. They wanted the government to spend less money. Obama had said the federal government would help homeowners facing foreclosure. Many people were angry. The government had already spent billions of dollars bailing out failing businesses. And the country was in debt. This led Rick Santelli of CNBC to call for a Chicago Tea Party. It would be a protest, taking its name from the Boston Tea Party, which led to the American Revolutionary War.

The Tea Party's first big protest was on Tax Day, April 15, 2009. Tax Day is the deadline for filing personal income tax returns. More than 250,000 people protested in Washington, DC, and around the country. They carried tea bags and signs that protested government spending. Some people thought the government was not responsible with how it spent tax dollars. Small business owners were worried that the tax raises would shut them down.

That month, Obama responded to the Tea Party's concerns over the national debt. He said he inherited the debt. He said any spending he approved was needed for the economy. But the Tea Party continued to oppose too much government spending, high taxes, and rising debt.

The Tea Party had another goal. They thought the Republican Party was not conservative enough. So Tea Party candidates competed against Republicans in elections. The Tea Party influenced the 2010 midterms. Dozens of Tea Party-backed candidates won seats in Congress. These wins helped Republicans take control of the House. It reduced the number of Democrats in the Senate.

Then, in May 2013, the Internal Revenue Service (IRS) said it was going to investigate groups that had applied for tax-exempt status. Groups of many political ties had applied for this status. But one-third of the organizations the IRS targeted had words such as "Tea Party" and "Patriots" in their names. Tea Party members accused the government of unfair treatment. The US Treasury Department reviewed the claim. They found no solid evidence of wrongdoing. But the Tea Party remained suspicious.

That same year, the Tea Party made a big push to defund the ACA. The last approved government funding bill only lasted until September 30. Congress needed to pass a bill that would decide government funding for the next several months. Tea Party members in the House proposed bills that funded the government. They would also defund the ACA. Democrats in the Senate rejected these bills. Neither side

OCCUPY WALL STREET

On September 17, 2011, protesters gathered in Zuccotti Park. It is in New York City's financial district in Manhattan. The people were protesting the power large banks and companies had. Protesters considered themselves the 99 percent that did not have great wealth. As a result, they believed they did not have influence in the country. The first night, approximately 100 protesters slept in the park. Within a month, more than 1,600 occupations sprang up in other cities. The occupation later influenced the Black Lives Matter movement. Its themes were also present in Bernie Sanders's campaign in the 2016 presidential election.

would work together. On October 1, the government partially shut down. Nonessential government agencies could not work because they did not have a budget.

The House Republicans created a budget to fund some agencies. Obama refused to sign any bill unless every agency reopened. If they couldn't come to an agreement by October 17, the United States would not be able to pay its loans. Eventually, the Tea Party compromised and created a plan. Obama signed it just before the deadline.

In 2014, the Tea Party's support weakened. Yet after the 2014 midterms, Republicans regained control of both chambers of Congress. And the Republican Party was more conservative than before. At the same time, people were still unsatisfied with the Republican Party. This opened the door for nontraditional Republican candidates to enter the 2016 presidential race.

STRAIGHT TO THE
SOURCE

The Tea Party was vocal in its complaints about the government. At a 2009 rally, Tom McClintock, a congressman from California, outlined some of these criticisms:

> We, as a people, are awakening to the danger of a government that spends too much and borrows too much and taxes too much, because we know what that means. We know that you can't spend your way rich. We know that you can't borrow your way out of debt. And we know that you can't tax your way to prosperity. No nation in the history of the world has ever spent, borrowed, and taxed its way to economic health.

Source: "Tea Party Rally." *Congressman Tom McClintock*. US House of Representatives, April 21, 2009. Web. Accessed June 24, 2017.

Back It Up

The author of this passage is using evidence to support a point. Write a paragraph describing the point the author is making. Then write two or three pieces of evidence the author uses to make the point.

CHAPTER
THREE

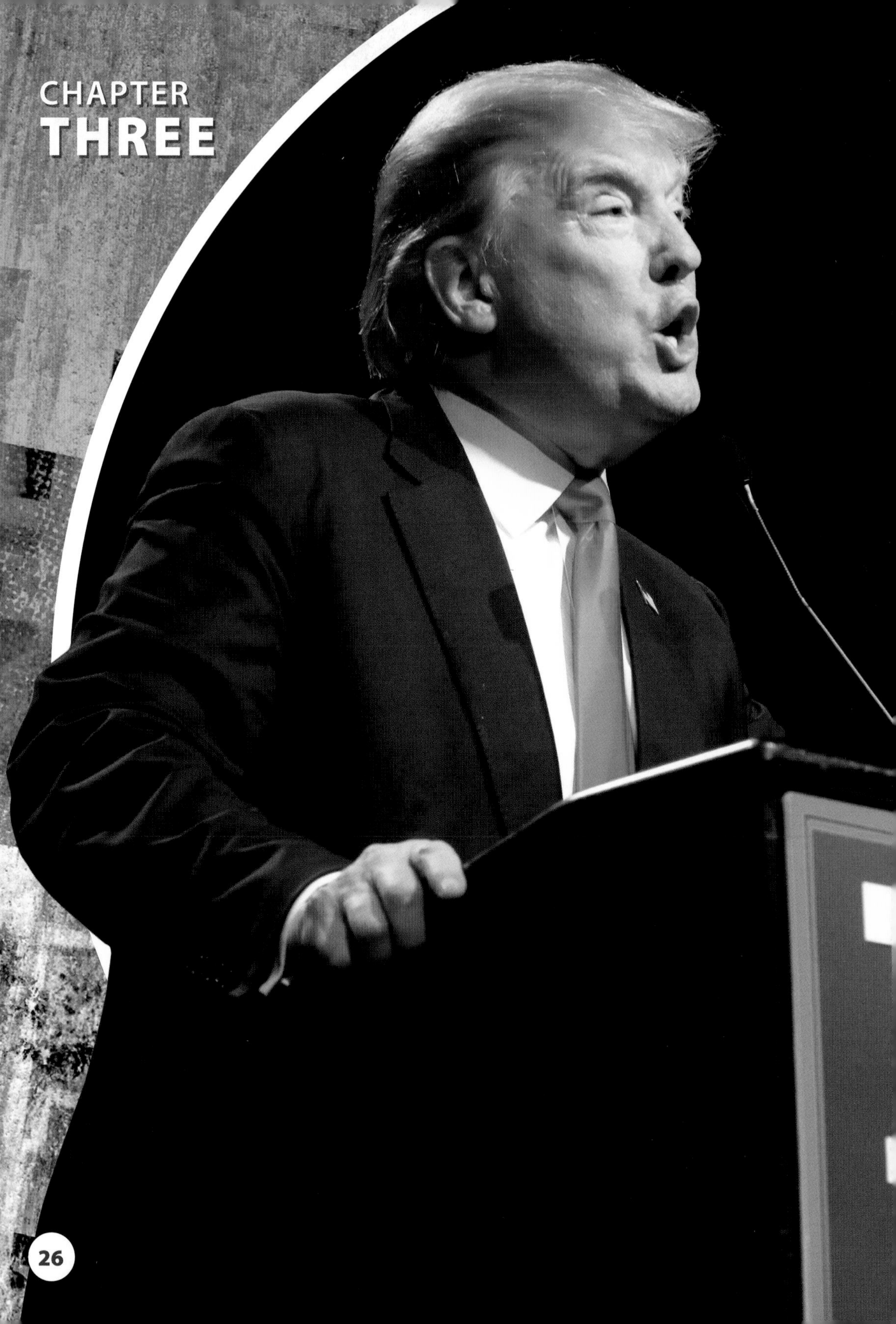

DONALD TRUMP FOR PRESIDENT

In the 2016 presidential election, voters looked for a different kind of candidate. They were sick of career politicians. In June 2015, Donald Trump said he was running for president. Trump, a well-known businessman and television personality, was not a typical candidate. He was not a politician.

Some did not think he was serious. Others wondered if he just wanted to win. As weeks turned into months, Trump's

Trump had considered running for president in 1999 but did not join the campaign for that election.

supporters grew. They were energized by some of his campaign promises.

CAMPAIGN PROMISES

Trump promised to "make America great again." Some people wanted to stop Mexican immigrants from illegally entering the country. Some voters without college degrees felt these people were taking jobs from them. Others believed they committed crimes. Trump said he would deport undocumented immigrants. He pledged to build a wall along the US-Mexico border, saying it would keep people from illegally entering the United States. Trump also wanted to replace the ACA. Some voters liked this idea. They did not like the high costs or the penalties for not having insurance. Americans were also concerned about terrorist attacks. There had been several smaller attacks in the country over the past few years. Trump said he would ban Muslims from entering the United States. He insisted this would make Americans safer.

Trump's campaign rallies were often the site of heated protests.

A lot of supporters attended Trump's rallies. So did protesters. Trump said things that made people angry. He was also accused of objectifying women. Some protests turned violent. In May 2016, people protesting Trump in Albuquerque, New Mexico, threw burning T-shirts and bottles at police.

Trump supporters also caused trouble. Critics blamed Trump for the behavior of his supporters.

TRUMP SUPPORTERS

The resistance to Trump began as soon as he announced his candidacy. But he also had support from the start. There were many reasons voters supported Trump. Some liked his straightforward way of talking. Others said they were tired of career politicians. Although he was wealthy, some said he behaved like a regular guy.

They said he encouraged it. At a rally in Iowa, Trump told the crowd that protesters might throw tomatoes. He said it was okay to attack the protesters. He even offered to pay legal fees if they were arrested. And critics accused him of blaming victims. When a protester was assaulted in Alabama, Trump said he might have deserved it. But Trump's aggressive nature also earned him supporters.

VICTORY AND RESISTANCE

On November 8, 2016, Trump won the election. Resistance to the new president began immediately.

Thousands of students across the country held protests. In New York, thousands huddled at Trump's skyscraper, Trump Tower. More than 1,000 high school students protested at the city hall in Los Angeles, California. In Washington, DC, more than 2,000 students protested in front of Trump International Hotel. They participated because of Trump's proposed policies on immigration.

Some rejected statements he made about women. Most worried his policies could negatively affect their futures. People also turned to social media to organize protests. They voiced their worries about a Trump presidency. Hashtags including

STUDENT WALKOUTS

The Tuesday after Trump won the election, students in Washington, DC, walked out of school. They gathered around Trump International Hotel carrying signs and chanting. They weren't old enough to vote. It was their way of letting Trump know what they wanted. Several schools supported the protest. Some teachers and other school workers went with the students to keep them safe.

WOMEN'S MARCH ON WASHINGTON

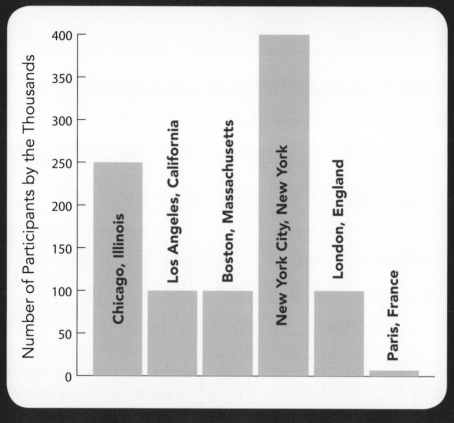

Many protesters participated in "sister" marches on the day of the Women's March on Washington. This bar graph shows the number of participants from six of the marches. Why do you think some cities had more protesters than others?

#NotMyPresident and #ImStillWithHer (referring to Clinton) became popular.

INAUGURAL RESISTANCE

Celebrities boycotted the inauguration. Sixty-seven Democratic members of Congress also skipped it. Crowds along parts of the parade route were thin. Protests sprang up across the country. Most marches were peaceful. A few became violent. In Washington, DC, demonstrators threw rocks at the police and smashed windows. One set a limousine on fire. More than 200 people were arrested. The day after, the Women's March took place.

FURTHER EVIDENCE

Chapter Three talks about reasons people either supported or resisted Trump. What was one of the main points of the chapter? What evidence supports this point? Read the article on the website below. Does the information support the main point of the chapter? Does it present new evidence?

USA TODAY: TRUMP NATION

abdocorelibrary.com/political-resistance

WOMEN'S
RIGHTS
are
HUMAN
RIGHTS

RESISTANCE TO TRUMP'S PRESIDENCY

fter the Women's March on Washington, resistance to the new president continued. Organizers planned "A Day without a Woman" for March 8, 2017. Women and supporters were asked to not go to work. Shopping was discouraged, unless it was at a woman- or minority-owned business. Supporters were asked to wear red in support of the movement.

Some women held rallies outside of the House of Representatives on A Day without a Woman.

LETTER, E-MAIL, AND PHONE RESISTANCE

Activists encouraged protesters to use their pen or keyboard to resist Trump. One movement asked people to send postcards to the president on March 15, 2017. Some sent postcards to express their anger at Trump's policies. Others were frustrated with Trump personally. Approximately one million postcards were sent.

Voters also flooded Republican politicians with e-mails, letters, and phone calls. They hoped that politicians would support their positions in the government.

RESISTANCE TO TRUMP'S POLICIES

President Trump has tried to keep some immigrants from entering the United States. On January 27, 2017, he signed an executive order. It kept Syrian refugees from entering the United States. It also temporarily kept citizens from seven Muslim-majority countries from coming to the United States. Trump said he wanted time to review the screening process. He hoped to prevent another terrorist attack. Critics said it was religious discrimination. They argued the screening process was already thorough. They said rejecting people seeking help was not the answer to fighting terrorism. After the president's order, popular hashtags including #NoBanNoWall and #MuslimBan trended. People filled airports to protest. Several federal judges blocked the order. Immigration advocates also fought it. In response to this resistance, Trump released a revision on June 30. People from those countries could now come to the United States. But they needed a

REPLACING THE ACA

Trump pledged to replace the ACA during his first 100 days in office. In early March 2017, the American Health Care Act was presented to the House. But the bill was pulled. Republicans did not have enough votes for it to pass. Some people worried insurance costs would rise. Others feared pre-existing health conditions would not be covered. The plan was revised and sent back to the House. Many citizens continued to protest the proposed changes.

GETTING INVOLVED

The Women's March on Washington created a Youth Ambassador Program. The youngest ambassador is nine-year-old Mari Copeny. Mari is "Little Miss Flint," known for bringing attention to the water crisis in Flint, Michigan. The crisis began in 2014 after the city changed their water supply to the Flint River. Errors at the treatment facility contaminated the water supply. This caused health issues. Residents must use bottled water for most of their needs. The young advocate posted on Twitter, "One day I will change the world but until then I'll take clean water."

family connection or to be attending a school or working at a business. Trump issued a new travel ban in September, and people continued to fight to lift the bans.

RACIAL TENSIONS

On August 12, 2017, violence erupted in Charlottesville, Virginia. The city was going to take down a Confederate statue. The Confederacy fought for slavery during the American Civil War (1861–1865).

MUSLIM-MAJORITY COUNTRY EXECUTIVE ORDER

Trump's first proposed immigration halt targeted seven countries. The map above shows these countries. What do you know about these countries? Why do you think some Americans were upset with the order?

White supremacists, who think white people are better than others, came to protest. Some had weapons. Some had flags with Nazi symbols. A Nazi is someone who agrees with Adolf Hitler's Nazi Party regime, which ruled Germany before and during World War II (1939–1945). Many other people came to counter this protest. The protesters and counter protesters clashed, and several were injured. The violence escalated when a Nazi sympathizer drove a car into a crowd of the

People in New York City protest the immigration ban.

counter protesters, killing one. Trump spoke against the violence. But many people were angry when he did not specifically speak against racism. They felt he was blaming both sides equally. People continued to protest racism and Trump's response in the following days.

THE FUTURE OF THE MOVEMENT

The current resistance is a grassroots movement. It is run by different organizations and individuals. Some help young people run for local offices. By winning these offices, candidates gain experience. They can then run for more prominent offices. Americans can make a difference in politics. Organizers continue to fight for causes they believe in. The current political resistance movement shows no signs of slowing down.

STRAIGHT TO THE
SOURCE

Ten days before Trump's inauguration, President Obama delivered his farewell speech. In it, he encouraged citizens to become more engaged. In his speech, he said:

> *So, you see, that's what our democracy demands. It needs you. Not just when there's an election, not just when your own narrow interest is at stake, but over the full span of a lifetime. If you're tired of arguing with strangers on the Internet, try talking with one of them in real life. If something needs fixing, then lace up your shoes and do some organizing. If you're disappointed by your elected officials, grab a clipboard, get some signatures, and run for office yourself. Show up. Dive in. Stay at it.*

> Source: "Remarks by the President in Farewell Address." *The White House: President Barack Obama*. US National Archives and Records Administration, January 10, 2017. Web. Accessed May 7, 2017.

Consider Your Audience

Adapt the president's message for a different audience, such as your parents or friends. Write a blog post conveying the same ideas for your new audience. How is your message different from the original text and why?

FAST FACTS

- People become politically active. Citizens seek to influence elected officials, changing their policies and decisions.

- Key players include American citizens who are dissatisfied with a politician or policy, the Tea Party, Teresa Shook, Bob Bland, Tamika Mallory, Carmen Perez, and Linda Sarsour.

- Activists resisted President George W. Bush because they said the Supreme Court, not the people, decided he won the 2000 election. They did not agree with the wars and government bailouts during his two terms in office.

- Much of the resistance to President Barack Obama was because of the Affordable Care Act. Others blamed him for high taxes and rising debt.

- Many opposed President Donald Trump because of what they perceived as racist and sexist comments. They also opposed many of his policies, including immigration restrictions.

- The Women's March provided a way for people's voices to be heard.

- In response to resistance, Trump revised an executive order on immigration, making it more lenient, and later issued a new travel ban.

IMPORTANT DATES

2003
On March 20, the United States invades Iraq.

2009
On April 15, the Tea Party has its first major protest.

2010
The Affordable Care Act is signed into law on March 23.

2013
On October 1, the US government partially shuts down when Democratic and Republican members of Congress cannot agree on a budget.

2017
On January 20, Donald Trump is inaugurated as the 45th US president. On January 21, the Women's March on Washington takes place. And on January 27, Trump signs an executive order halting immigration from seven Muslim-majority countries. Trump revises this executive order on June 30, making it more lenient. He then issued a new travel ban in September.

STOP AND
THINK

Tell the Tale
Chapter One of this book discusses the Women's March on Washington. Imagine you plan to participate in a march for an issue you are passionate about. Write 200 words about the march and why you plan to participate.

Surprise Me
This book discusses ways protesters have demonstrated against the government. After reading this book, what two or three facts about their demonstrations surprised you the most? Write a sentence about each fact. Why did you find each fact surprising?

Dig Deeper
After reading this book, what questions do you still have about political resistance? With an adult's help, find a few reliable sources that can help answer your questions. Write a paragraph about what you learned.

GLOSSARY

bail out
to provide funding to save a person or company from money problems

boycott
to no longer deal with a business, organization, or person as a way of protesting

defund
to cut funding for something

foreclosure
when a bank reclaims a property because the owner has missed too many payments

grassroots
run by ordinary people instead of political leaders

inauguration
an event to officially place someone in office

LGBTQ
an acronym for people who identify as lesbian, gay, bisexual, transgender, or queer or questioning

reform
to improve or change for the better

refugee
someone who leaves his or her country for another because of concerns for his or her safety

weapon of mass destruction
a weapon that can kill many people at once, such as a chemical or nuclear weapon

ONLINE
RESOURCES

To learn more about political resistance today, visit our free resource websites below.

Visit **abdocorelibrary.com** for free Common Core resources for teachers and students, including vetted activities, multimedia, and booklinks, for deeper subject comprehension.

Visit **abdobooklinks.com** for free additional online weblinks for further learning. These links are routinely monitored and updated to provide the most current information available.

LEARN
MORE

Hinman, Bonnie. *Donald Trump: 45th President of the United States*. Minneapolis, MN: Abdo Publishing, 2017.

Parker, Philip. *The Presidents Visual Encyclopedia*. New York: DK Publishing, 2017.

ABOUT THE
AUTHORS

Duchess Harris, JD, PhD

Professor Harris is the chair of the American Studies Department at Macalester College. The author and coauthor of four books (*Hidden Human Computers: The Black Women of NASA* and *Black Lives Matter* with Sue Bradford Edwards, *Racially Writing the Republic: Racists, Race Rebels, and Transformations of American Identity* with Bruce Baum, and *Black Feminist Politics from Kennedy to Clinton/Obama*), she has been an associate editor for *Litigation News*, the American Bar Association Section's quarterly flagship publication, and was the first editor-in-chief of *Law Raza Journal*, an interactive online race and the law journal for William Mitchell College of Law.

She has earned a PhD in American Studies from the University of Minnesota and a Juris Doctorate from William Mitchell College of Law.

Myra Faye Turner

Myra Faye Turner is a writer, poet, and children's book author. She lives in New Orleans, Louisiana, with her teenage son. She enjoys learning new facts. She has never missed a presidential election while she has been eligible to vote.

INDEX